Table of Contents

Essential Question

What compels us to survive?

Notes

Androcles and the Lion

by Aesop

Androcles, who escaped from slavery, comes face-to-face with a man-eating lion two times in this story. How will he survive this life-threatening situation?

1   Back in the days of the Roman Empire, Androcles escaped from his master and then fled into the deep, dark forest. While wandering about in the dense woods, he came upon a lion lying down and loudly moaning and groaning. At first Androcles turned to flee, but finding that the lion did not pursue him, he turned back and went up to the beast. As he came near, the lion put out his paw, which was swollen and bleeding. Androcles found that a huge thorn had got into the paw, and that was causing the lion's pain. Androcles pulled out the thorn and then bound up the paw of the lion. The grateful cat rose and, not unlike a house pet, licked the hand of Androcles.

2   Then the lion took Androcles to his cave. Every day he brought Androcles meat, which filled Androcles's stomach. But shortly afterward, both Androcles and the lion were captured and sent to the city to be part of the public spectacle.

3 Androcles was sentenced to be thrown to the lion in front of the emperor and all his court. Meanwhile, the poor lion had been kept without food for several days, so he was ravenous, and all thought he would devour Androcles in an instant. The time came, and Androcles was led into the middle of the arena. Soon the lion was let loose from his den, and rushed bounding and roaring toward his victim. But as soon as the lion came near to Androcles, he recognized his friend. The lion fawned upon him, and licked his hands lovingly. The emperor, surprised at this, summoned Androcles to him. Androcles then told him about how he had helped the lion by removing the thorn. Whereupon the emperor pardoned and freed the brave man, and let the lion loose in his native forest.

Notes

Brushfire!

a play excerpt

by David Boelke

During "fire season" in Southern California, hot desert winds can blow sparks from wildfires into the bone-dry canyons and valleys of inhabited areas. Thousands of acres of land burn as the blazes light up the night sky. Despite firefighters' heroic efforts, deadly whirlwinds of flames and intense heat called "firenados" add to the chaos as the devastation rages on.

Cast of Characters

Ed Acosta: A driven film composer

Meg Acosta: Ed's wife and mother to Jack and Samantha

Jack Acosta: The Acostas' twelve-year-old son

Mike Peters: A tough but fair veteran firefighter

Setting

The Acostas' hillside home in Clarita Canyon, a suburb of Los Angeles. Late spring. Downstage is ED's music room; upstage, behind a sliding screen door, is a wooden deck. A burning mountain can be seen in the background. Lighting effects establish that fires are burning there; they get increasingly closer during the scene.

(ED sits at his piano, talking on a cell phone. MEG rushes around, carrying photo albums and boxes.)

ED: I'm telling you, Manny. The opening number is pure gold. Listen. *(He plays a tune.)* What did I tell you?

MEG: Ed, why aren't you loading the car? (*The house phone rings. MEG answers.*) Acostas' residence. Yes. (*To ED, her hand over the mouthpiece*) The fire department is telling us to evacuate. The Sorensons' place down the hill is already a pile of ashes. (*To caller*) No, no need to send anyone, we're just getting in the car.

ED: (*Playing another tune into the cell phone*) We're going to need strings here, Manny.

MEG: Where's Jack? Jack!

JACK: (*Enters from outside*) What is it, Mom?

MEG: Have you loaded your laptop? Your suitcase! Tell me you packed your suitcase!

JACK: Packed and in the car.

MEG: Where's Samantha?

JACK: Out looking for Augie.

MEG: No! No, no, no! We have no time to find that crazy dog. Go and find your sister. Now! (*JACK exits through deck; she looks outside.*) Ed! I'm seeing a plume of smoke coming from next door. Those flames are moving like race cars! Right at us!

ED: I'll have to get back to you, Manny. (*He hangs up the phone, turns to MEG.*) Why all the drama, Meg? We've survived twenty years of brushfires up here. Now if you'll let me be, fifty musicians are showing up at the studio to record my music tomorrow . . . 9 a.m. . . . sharp!

MEG: Have you looked outside? The hillside is in flames.

ED: *(Looks out window, calm)* Awesome! Too bad I'm not writing music for a disaster movie. Ha! *(Pauses; SFX of helicopter gets louder.)* That chopper is coming our way.

MIKE: *(Offstage, through a loudspeaker, over helicopter sounds)* Attention, residents! This is Mike Peters from the L.A.F.D. This is your final warning. Vacate your homes and head to the Rescue Center at the Clarita Canyon Mall.

MEG: Hear that? We don't have a choice.

ED: Oh, please. You're such a drama queen. Look. The cavalry has arrived! Fire planes are dropping chemicals on the Stadler house. *(He goes back to playing piano.)*

MEG: *(Slamming the lid down on the keyboard)* This . . . is . . . not . . . a . . . MOVIE! The Changs down the ravine lost their house in the time it took those planes to reload and get back here. You can feel the heat from the flames! Get whatever matters to you in the van . . . now!

ED: What matters to me is this piano.

MEG: You're going to put yourself in danger for a beat-up piano? Not me! *(She turns from ED and addresses JACK as he enters.)* Where's Sam?

JACK: In the car—with Augie—looking for her stuffed bunny. Dad, I'm begging you. Come with us.

ED: *(Ignoring Jack)* "Beat-up piano"? Three generations of Acostas have banged out a living on this thing and I'm not leaving it behind for flames, looters, or vandals.

MEG: Ed, we're leaving—with you or without you.

ED: I'm telling you that they've got it under control. You know these L.A. firefighters. If I leave, it could be days before they let me back here to work. This movie is my big break, but I've got a ton of work to do before tomorrow. I'll keep the roof wet with the hose and watch out for sparks.

MIKE: (*Offstage*) Attention, Baker Drive residents. You must evacuate immediately!

(*ED shakes his head, resumes playing piano. The music is sad.*)

MEG: What good is winning an Oscar if you're not around to enjoy it? Priorities, Eduardo. (*She kisses him on the forehead and pauses at the door.*) Priorities. (*MEG and JACK exit. ED continues playing, not noticing the fire coming closer; sparks ignite the deck outside.*)

ED: Uh-oh!

(*He rushes through the sliding door, grabs the hose, aims it at the flames and turns on the tap. All that comes out is dust.*)

ED: Unbelievable. They must have diverted the water to fight the fire. . . . Now what?

(*The sound of a helicopter gets louder, then fades away as the lights fade to black.*)

set designer's sketch for the
Acostas' music room/deck

Notes

Sinbad and the Valley of Diamonds

Sinbad the Sailor is the hero of Arabian folktales. He undertakes seven voyages. In this installment, Sinbad's ship accidentally left him behind on an island inhabited by a roc, a gigantic legendary bird. Sinbad uses his turban to bind himself to the roc's huge leg. When the bird takes flight, it transports Sinbad to a valley of diamonds.

1   I had always believed the stories about a valley of diamonds were tall tales. Now, to my amazement, everywhere I looked I saw diamonds! My delight was speedily dampened when I realized the valley was also home to serpents with jaws large enough to swallow a man whole. I was desperate to escape, but the valley was surrounded by high, steep mountains.

2   Fortunately, the serpents stayed in caves during the day. At night, when they emerged to stalk their prey, I hid inside a cave and blocked the entrance. The next day huge pieces of raw meat were launched into the valley from the cliffs above. I realized that another part of the stories was true. According to the tales, merchants acquired the diamonds by means of nesting eagles. The gems stuck to the meat that eagles carried to their nests high above for their chicks. There, the merchants gathered the diamonds.

3   I immediately saw an opportunity to escape. After storing several diamonds in my leather bag, I strapped a lump of meat to my back. As I had hoped, an eagle seized the meat and me with it, and flew up to its nest. The merchants came upon me and at first were furious, because they thought I was stealing their profits. However, they calmed down when I offered to share my treasure. I then traveled with my new acquaintances out of the mountains and returned to Baghdad.

BuildReflectWrite

Build Knowledge

What skills and character traits do the main characters use to survive their predicaments? Then choose one character who you think is most heroic, and explain why.

Story	Character	Skills/Traits	Most Heroic/Why
Androcles and the Lion	Androcles		
Androcles and the Lion	Lion		
Brushfire!	Ed		

Reflect

What compels us to survive?

Based on this week's texts, write down new ideas and questions you have about the essential question.

_____

_____

_____

_____

_____

_____

Building Research Skills

Narrative

Imagine that you have been asked to write a play involving a brushfire. One of your guiding research questions is: What are the causes of brushfires? Read and take notes from two or more sources to answer this question. List the sources of your information.

Notes

The Law of Club and Fang

an excerpt from *The Call of the Wild*

by Jack London

During the Alaskan gold rush of the late 1890s, dogs were in demand to pull sleds through the snow. Buck, the large pet dog of a Californian ranch family, is stolen and sold into slavery as a sled dog. He confronts basic survival throughout the novel, from dealing with the brutal weather to learning how to avoid beatings from humans and attacks from other dogs.

1   Buck's first day on the Dyea beach was like a nightmare. Every hour was filled with shock and surprise. He had been suddenly jerked from the heart of civilization and flung into the heart of things primordial[1]. No lazy, sun-kissed life was this, with nothing to do but loaf and be bored. Here was neither peace, nor rest, nor a moment's safety. All was confusion and action. Every moment life and limb were in peril. There was imperative need to be constantly alert. These dogs and men were not town dogs and men. They were savages, all of them, who knew no law but the law of club and fang.

1 primordial—primitive

12

2   He had never seen dogs fight as these wolfish creatures fought. And his first experience taught him an unforgettable lesson. It is true, it was a vicarious experience, else he would not have lived to profit by it. Curly was the victim. They were camped near the log store, where she, in her friendly way, made advances to a husky dog the size of a full-grown wolf, though not half so large as she. There was no warning. There was only a leap in like a flash, a metallic clip of teeth, a leap out equally swift, and Curly's face was ripped open from eye to jaw.

3   It was the wolf manner of fighting, to strike and leap away; but there was more to it than this. Thirty or forty huskies ran to the spot and surrounded the combatants in an intent and silent circle. Buck did not comprehend that silent intentness, nor the eager way with which they were licking their chops. Curly rushed her antagonist, who struck again and leaped aside. He met her next rush with his chest, in a peculiar fashion that tumbled her off her feet. She never regained them. This was what the onlooking huskies had waited for. They closed in upon her, snarling and yelping, and she was buried, screaming with agony, beneath the bristling mass of bodies.

4   So sudden was it, and so unexpected, that Buck was taken aback. He saw Spitz[2] run out his scarlet tongue in a way he had of laughing. He saw Francois[3], swinging an axe, spring into the mess of dogs. Three men with clubs were helping him to scatter them.

2 Spitz—the lead dog
3 Francois—the human owner of the dog team

5   It did not take long. Two minutes from the time Curly went down, the last of her assailants were clubbed off. But she lay there limp and lifeless in the bloody, trampled snow, almost literally torn to pieces. Francois was standing over her and cursing horribly. The scene often came back to Buck to trouble him in his sleep. So that was the way. No fair play. Once down, that was the end of you. Well, he would see to it that he never went down. Spitz ran out his tongue and laughed again, and from that moment Buck hated him with a bitter and deathless hatred.

6   Before he had recovered from the shock caused by the tragic passing of Curly, he received another shock. Francois fastened upon him an arrangement of straps and buckles.

15

7   It was a harness, such as he had seen the grooms put on the horses at home. And as he had seen horses work, so he was set to work. He hauled Francois on a sled to the forest that fringed the valley. Then he returned with a load of firewood.

8   Though his dignity was sorely hurt by thus being made a draught animal, he was too wise to rebel. He buckled down with a will and did his best, though it was all new and strange. Francois was stern, demanding instant obedience, and by virtue of his whip receiving instant obedience; while Dave, who was an experienced wheeler, nipped Buck's hindquarters whenever he was in error. Spitz was the leader, likewise experienced, and while he could not always get at Buck, he growled sharp reproof now and again, or cunningly threw his weight in the traces to jerk Buck into the way he should go.

Notes

9   Buck learned easily, and under the combined tuition of his two mates and Francois made remarkable progress. Ere they returned to camp he knew enough to stop at "ho," to go ahead at "mush," to swing wide on the bends, and to keep clear of the wheeler when the loaded sled shot downhill at their heels.

10   That night Buck faced the great problem of sleeping. The tent, illumined by a candle, glowed warmly in the midst of the white plain. When he entered it, both Perrault and Francois bombarded him with curses and cooking utensils. Buck recovered from his consternation and fled ignominiously into the outer cold. A chill wind was blowing that nipped him sharply and bit with especial venom into his wounded shoulder. He lay down on the snow and attempted to sleep, but the frost soon drove him shivering to his feet.

11   Miserable and disconsolate, he wandered about among the many tents, only to find that one place was as cold as another. Here and there savage dogs rushed upon him, but he bristled his neck hair and snarled. For he was learning fast, and they let him go his way unmolested.

12   Finally an idea came to him. He would return and see how his own teammates were making out. To his astonishment, they had disappeared. Again he wandered about through the great camp, looking for them, and again he returned. Were they in the tent? No, that could not be, else he would not have been driven out. Then where could they possibly be? With drooping tail and shivering body, very forlorn indeed, he aimlessly circled the tent. Suddenly the snow gave way beneath his forelegs and he sank down. Something wriggled under his feet. He sprang back, bristling and snarling, fearful of the unseen and unknown. But a friendly little yelp reassured him, and he went back to investigate. A whiff of warm air ascended to his nostrils, and there, curled up under the snow in a snug ball, lay Billee. He whined placatingly, squirmed and wriggled to show his goodwill and intentions, and even ventured, as a bribe for peace, to lick Buck's face with his warm wet tongue.

13   Another lesson. So that was the way they did it, eh? Buck confidently selected a spot, and with much fuss and waste effort proceeded to dig a hole for himself. In a trice the heat from his body filled the confined space and he was asleep. The day had been long and arduous, and he slept soundly and comfortably, though he growled and barked and wrestled with bad dreams.

Gold Rush!

1   Imagine my astonishment when Pa announced that he'd quit his job to go prospecting for gold. At first he intended to leave me behind, saying, "It's no place for a thirteen-year-old girl, Lillian." But ever since Ma died, it's been just the two of us. I begged him to take me along and he relented.

2   We started for the Klondike, a region in northwest Canada, in the summer of 1897. We didn't know it then, but it would take us an entire year to reach the goldfields.

3   A steamship took us north to Alaska. There, by order of the Canadian government, we gathered enough provisions to last us a year. Next, we set off on the Chilkoot Trail into Canada, carrying all our supplies on our backs.

4   The harsh Canadian winter was just weeks away. I looked at the mountains we'd have to traverse and shivered with apprehension.

5   As we struggled over a mountain pass, a blizzard blew in and visibility dropped to nearly zero. We inched our way blindly along the trail with the other would-be prospectors, as the snow scoured our faces and the wind howled.

6   After the blizzard passed, we forced our way through high snowdrifts. I gasped, horrified when I almost stepped on a frozen body. Pa said a prayer and hurried me ahead. "Poor fellow," he muttered. "Can't even bury him until the ground thaws next spring."

7   Exhaustion dogged my steps and I nearly gave up. But Pa chivvied me along until at last we reached the Yukon River and prepared to boat downriver to the Klondike and what I hoped would be our golden future.

BuildReflectWrite

Build Knowledge

List some of the problems Buck faced that threatened his survival. How did he solve them? Then discuss the type of character Buck is, and explain your reasoning.

Buck's Problems	Solutions

Reflect

What compels us to survive?

Based on this week's texts, jot down new ideas and questions you have about the essential question.

_____

_____

_____

_____

_____

_____

Building Research Skills

Informative/Explanatory

Imagine that you have been asked to write an informational essay about dogsled teams. One of your guiding research questions is: How have these dogsled teams helped humans survive in harsh climates? Read and take notes from at least two sources to answer this question. List the sources of your information.

Remember to annotate as you read.

Notes

Julie Fights for Survival

an excerpt from *Julie of the Wolves*

by Jean Craighead George

Julie, known as Miyax in her Eskimo village, age thirteen, has run away from an arranged marriage. She ends up lost in the Alaskan wilderness, where she learns to survive by observing, befriending, and finally becoming accepted by a pack of wolves. In the following section, the long, dark, and dangerous Arctic winter is settling in and her summer compound has been destroyed. Will she be able to get to the coast in time and onto a ship, or will she need to survive the winter in the wilderness?

1   Suddenly something moved. Julie bolted out of bed and grabbed her club. The grass crackled behind her and she spun around. Sedges[1] bobbed to say it was only the wind.

2   "Ayi!" She was disgusted by her fears. She kicked a stone to change something, since she could not change what she was doing, as Kapugen[2] advised.

1 sedge—grasslike plants that thrive in the tundra
2 Kapugen—Julie's father, a skilled hunter and trapper

3   Feeling better, she slid back in her sleeping skin. "I guess," she said to herself, "that the sun's been up so long I've forgotten the sounds of the night." As she waited for sleep she listened to the polar wind whistle, and the dry grasses whined like the voice of the old bent lady.

4   "Jello!"[3] she screamed, sitting bolt upright. He was almost beside her, his teeth bared as he growled. Then he picked up her pack and ran.

5   She jumped out of bed and started after him, for her very life was in that pack—food, needles, knives, even her boots.

3 Jello—a lone wolf that has tried to join the pack

6   The wind chilled her naked body and she stopped to collect her wits. She must act with wisdom. She must think! Her clothes, where were her clothes? They, too, were gone. No, she remembered they were safe in the bladder bag under the caribou skin.

7   Quickly she pulled them out and clutched them to her chest, but they were of little comfort. She could go nowhere without boots; nor could she make new ones. Her needles and ulo[4], the tools of survival, were all in the pack. Shivering, she slid into bed and cried. A tear fell on the grass and froze solid.

8   "My tombstone."

9   She lay very still wondering how long it would take for life to leave her.

10   When she opened her eyes it was daylight and the warm yellow of the land gave her hope. She could eat her caribou skin if she had to. Rolling to her stomach, she smelled something sweet and recognized the scent of wolf urine. It had been dropped at the edge of her bag and was frozen but fresh. Someone had greeted her during the night. It could not have been Jello for the scent did not have the bitter odor of an angry and desolate wolf. Furthermore, it was sparsely given, not the dousing given to hostile objects. It must have been Amaroq[5]. She sniffed again but her nose was not sensitive enough to read the other messages in the urine that meant "all is well." Yet its light and loving scent gave her a sense of security and she smiled at the sun, dressed, and put her mind to inventing boots.

4 ulo—a half-moon-shaped knife used primarily by Eskimo women
5 Amaroq—the wolf-pack leader

11   Wrapping the drag around one foot and her sleeping skin around the other, she clomped awkwardly through the grass in a wider and wider circle hoping that Jello, having eaten her meat, would have abandoned the pack. She did not care about the food anymore. Her ulo and needles and matches were more important to find. With them she could make shoes, hunt, and cook. She marveled at how valuable these simple things were, how beautiful and precious. With them she could make a home, a larder, a sled, and clothes. And the cold air was equally precious. With it she could, like her father, freeze leather and sinew into sleds, spears, and harpoons. She would not die here if she could find her ulo and needles.

12   As she carefully searched the ground she began to think about seal camp. The old Eskimos were scientists too.

13   By using the plants, animals, and temperature, they had changed the harsh Arctic into a home, a feat as incredible as sending rockets to the moon. She smiled. The people at seal camp had not been as outdated and old-fashioned as she had been led to believe. No, on the contrary, they had been wise. They adjusted to nature instead of to man-made gadgets.

14   "Ayi!" she gasped. On the side of a ground swell lay Jello, his body torn in bloody shreds, his face contorted. Beside him lay her backpack!

15   Instantly she knew what had happened; Amaroq had turned on him. Once Kapugen had told her that some wolves had tolerated a lone wolf until the day he stole meat from the pups. With that, the leader gave a signal and his pack turned, struck, and tore the lone wolf to pieces. "There is no room in the wolf society for an animal who cannot contribute," he had said.

16   Jello had been so cowed he was useless. And now he was dead.

17   Slowly she opened her pack. The food was gone but her needles, ulo, and boots were tucked in the pockets where she had put them. They were now more wonderful to Miyax than airplanes, ocean liners, and great wide bridges. As she put on her shoes she checked for her man's knife and matches. They were there, too. Life was hers again! Slinging her pack to her shoulders, she placed a stone at Jello's head and turned away.

18   "You've got to be a super-wolf to live," she said. "Poor Jello was not." She left him to the Jaegers and foxes.

19   "Amaroq, wolf, my friend," she sang as she walked along. "Amaroq, my adopted father."

20   Reaching Point Hope seemed less important, now that she had come to truly understand the value of her ulo and needles. If she missed the boat she could live well until another year. Her voice rang out happily as she sang and followed the birds and her compass.

Remember to annotate as you read.

Notes

Survival in the Arctic

In 2003, explorer Pen Hadow became the first person to trek 770 kilometers (478 miles) solo from Canada to the Geographic North Pole. This was an extraordinary feat that took more than two months. Temperatures in the Arctic can be as low as –40 degrees Celsius (–40 degrees Fahrenheit). Polar winds can make it feel even colder. Would you like to take on such a far-flung adventure? Here is Hadow's advice to ensure your well-being.

1   1. Wear at least four layers of warm, breathable clothing. Choose thermal underwear and fleece that dry quickly. It's important to keep yourself both warm and dry. Excess moisture freezes instantly.

2   2. Take a sleeping bag designed for extreme cold. A bag fitted with an inflatable thermal mattress will keep you off the ice, so you stay warm and dry all night.

3   3. Watch for symptoms of frostbite. Extreme cold turns your skin chalky white due to tissue damage. The body parts most likely to be affected are the nose, cheeks, ears, and toes. Warm headgear will help you avoid frostbite. Wear mittens rather than gloves and lace your work boots loosely. These measures will improve blood flow to your hands and feet.

4   4. Keep your body fueled with meals and snacks that are high in calories. You need to eat and drink more than usual in the Arctic. Even ordinary tasks take extra effort in the cold, harsh environment. Add sports drinks and foods high in fat to your daily diet. Snacks that are ready-made, like nuts and chocolate, are also good on-the-go fuel.

5   5. Travel with someone. You will be able to watch out for each other.

6   6. Finally, if you encounter a polar bear, don't panic. A bright, loud flare should frighten it off.

7   Happy trekking!

BuildReflectWrite

Build Knowledge

What facts would you select to support the following analysis of Julie's character: she is brave and resourceful. Then determine one more character trait and defend it with information from the story.

Julie's Character	Evidence
brave	
resourceful	
other trait	

Reflect

What compels us to survive?

Based on this week's texts, write down new ideas and questions you have about the essential question.

_____

_____

_____

_____

_____

_____

Building Research Skills

Opinion

At the end of "Julie Fights for Survival," Julie is confident that, even if she misses the boat, she'll be able to survive the Arctic winter. Do you agree or disagree? Imagine that you have been asked to answer this question in an opinion essay. One of your guiding questions is: What are conditions like in the Arctic during the winter? Read and take notes from at least two sources to help you answer this question. List the sources of your information.

Support for Collaborative Conversation

Discussion Prompts

Express ideas or opinions . . .

When I read _____, it made me think that _____.

Based on the information in _____, my [opinion/idea] is _____.

As I [listened to/read/watched] _____, it occurred to me that _____.

It was important that _____.

Gain the floor . . .

I would like to add a comment. _____.

Excuse me for interrupting, but _____.

That made me think of _____.

Build on a peer's idea or opinion . . .

That's an interesting point. It makes me think _____.

If _____, then maybe _____.

[Name] said _____. That could mean that _____.

Express agreement with a peer's idea . . .

I agree that _____ because _____.

I also feel that _____ because _____.

[Name] made the comment that _____, and I think that is important because _____.

Respectfully express disagreement . . .

I understand your point of view that _____, but in my opinion _____ because _____.

That is an interesting idea, but did you consider the fact that _____?

I do not agree that _____. I think that _____ because _____.

Ask a clarifying question . . .

You said _____. Could you explain what you mean by that?

I don't understand how your evidence supports that inference. Can you say more?

I'm not sure I understand. Are you saying that _____?

Clarify for others . . .

When I said _____, what I meant was that _____.

I reached my conclusion because _____.

Group Roles

Discussion Director:
Your role is to guide the group's discussion and be sure that everyone has a chance to express his or her ideas.

Notetaker:
Your job is to record the group's ideas and important points of discussion.

Summarizer:
In this role, you will restate the group's comments and conclusions.

Presenter:
Your role is to provide an overview of the group's discussion to the class.

Timekeeper:
You will track the time and help to keep your peers on task.

Making Meaning with Words

Word	My Definition	My Sentence
adjusted (p. 27)		
ascended (p. 18)		
bolted (p. 22)		
chaos (p. 6)		
evacuate (p. 7)		
hostile (p. 24)		
marveled (p. 26)		
peril (p. 12)		
priorities (p. 9)		
vicarious (p. 13)		

Lexile 790L–960L

Build Knowledge Across 10 Topic Strands

Government and Citizenship

The U.S. Constitution: **Then** and **Now**

Character

Developing **Characters' Relationships**

Life Science
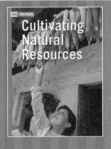
Cultivating Natural Resources

Point of View

Recognizing **Author's Point of View**

Technology and Society

Technology's **Impact** on Society

Theme

Up Against the **Wild**

History and Culture
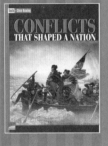
CONFLICTS THAT SHAPED A NATION

Earth Science
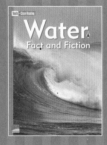
Water Fact and Fiction

Economics
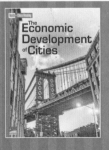
The **Economic Development** of Cities

Physical Science

Transforming **Matter**

Benchmark
UNIVERSE.COM™
BENCHMARK EDUCATION COMPANY

Grade 5 • Unit 6

ISBN 978-1-4900-9210-2

9 781490 092102